TUBESTARTER

Starting A Successful YouTube Channel

Devin Street

OEM Publishing

Published by Online Entrepreneurs Media Publishing, LLC.

Street, Devin

Tubestarter: Starting A Successful YouTube Channel

This book is available at a special discount when purchased in bulk for premiums and sales promotions as well as for fundraising and educational use. Special editions or updated versions of this book may also be available in the future at a discounted price with proof of purchase of this book. For more information, contact Online Entrepreneurs Media Publishing, LLC.

Devin Street is directly affiliated with Online Entrepreneurs Media Publishing, LLC. and earns more revenue from a purchase of his book than other authors associated with Online Entrepreneurs Media Publishing, LLC.

If you are interested in having your book published by Online Entrepreneurs Media Publishing, LLC. then please contact the company along with an attached file of the book you want to publish for review.

Table of Contents

About The Author

Well, it may be surprising but, I'm a 17-year-old high school student. I know right? You're probably thinking "Why should I listen to some high school student tell me how to build a YouTube channel?" Well since I was around 11 I've been experimenting on YouTube with many failed YouTube channels with only one or two successes before I finally decided to take a hiatus from YouTube to study and research exactly how YouTube turns normal average people into online millionaire stars throughout algorithm and research papers. Along with my own research and experiments, I was helped by Derral Eves, Tim Smycomer, Nick Nimmin, Brian G Johnson, and Roberto Blake to learn exactly how to trigger the YouTube algorithm to get the best results on YouTube. I then began creating niche YouTube channels I would grow and sell for profit. Fast forward to late Spring of 2017, where I finally decided to start a new channel for my personal brand. The only problem was that I didn't know what I wanted to create. I knew I had to create a channel that I was passionate about. I thought about doing a channel about Entrepreneurship or Marketing, which I still want to do one day, but finally decided I knew so much about YouTube, Facebook, Instagram, Twitter, WordPress, and social media marketing, that I should create a channel on growing and making money online and on social media. And then my mission statement finally came to me, "Helping you build an online presence and make money in the process." I thought it was perfect and apparently everyone else did also as now I have earned tens of thousands of views and subscribers on YouTube and plenty of followers and likes on Instagram. Which leads up to this point, the creation of my first book.

Dedicated to my friends, Ian, Razvan, Ryan, Aden, Matthew, Damon, and Nate, and every supporter of my channel and me, even if you have only watched one video.
And you the reader.

1. Creating A Channel

The first step to starting a successful YouTube channel is simply to create a channel. In the first section of this book you will learn how to create a YouTube channel properly and all the steps you will have to take before you post your first video.

1.1 Creating a Google account

An important thing you have to consider is your Google account itself. A Google account is so important because your Google account will connect you to everything. Gmail, Google Play Store, Drive, Calendars, Google Photos, Contacts, Hangouts, Google Wallets, Google Docs, Google Plus, Google AdSense, and most importantly, YouTube. As you can see, your Google account connects to everything you can imagine and it's important that you are not using a Google account for work, school, or personal use. The Google account you want to make will be specifically just for your YouTube channel and online brand, NOT for personal use. Now that you understand why you need to make a new account just for your YouTube channel, let's learn how to make one. The easiest way to do this is going to www.google.com, then clicking "sign in", and then click Create account. Once you get to the sign-up page you will want to enter your legal name, then one of the most important parts of creating your Google account, choosing an email username. When you create this you need to consider this is the main way your audience and businesses will contact you, until you eventually create a website, so you will want to have something easy to remember. When creating an email username you will likely want to use your name, the name of your brand name, or the name of your YouTube channel. If any of those are not available try something close using abbreviations. For instance, my name and channel name is "Devin Street" but the Gmail address "devinstreet@gmail.com" was already taken, so instead I chose "iamdevinstreet@gmail.com." After that be sure to enter your legal date of birth and cell phone number and then verify your account via voice call or text message. Now you have created your new Google account for your YouTube.

1.2 Creating A YouTube Channel

It you want to start a successful YouTube channel then you first have to at least have a channel created. The first thing you will need to do is head to youtube.com and click sign-in at the top right corner. Then, sign-in with the Google account that you just created. Next, what you need to do is click on your profile picture circle in the top right corner and click "Settings", a test icon. Under the settings you should see highlighted clickable text that says "Create A Channel" beside your email address for your new Google account. You will need to click that. A box should appear with the option for naming your channel. If you want your channel to be your first and last name then it should already be shown to you but if it is incorrect then just do a slight edit and "Create Channel" but if you don't want your channel to be your first and last name then you will need to select the "Use a business or other name" button. After selecting that, you will be lead to a new page to enter your channel name.

Choosing a channel name is extremely important and if you want to go more in-depth on the topic, click **here** to be taken to that chapter and section. Once you have selected your name, you will need to choose a category for your channel. If you will be using your YouTube channel to sell a product you make or extend your existing brand on a new platform, then select **Product or Brand.** If your YouTube channel is being created for a business or company, then select **Company Institution or Organization.** If you are creating your YouTube channel for entertainment purpose, for instance music, acting, comedy, gaming, or vlogging, then you will want to select **Arts, Entertainment, & Sports.** And if it does not fall into any of the above categories, like educational purposes, then select **Other.** Also, remember when you create this channel that Google will automatically create the channel a Google+ account. Next, read through and agree to the **Page Terms.** Then click **Done.** Great job, you just created your YouTube channel!

1.3 Logo & Header

Once you created a channel, you have to add the essentials to make it your own personal channel that separates you from everyone else, a logo and banner. When creating your logo and banner, you want something simple but intrigues people to want to subscribe. The last thing you want to do is have so many things it becomes confusing to the person and could actually be the decision maker on whether they subscribe or not. When creating a logo, it's important in how you design it. This will be the signature for your brand and will be used for everything from your own merchandise to your brand being brought up by other influencers. The last thing you want to do is base your logo on someone else's or even try to copy it. I recommend not even using pictures from online unless they are copyright free. The best decision to stay out of trouble is to make your logo from scratch. You will want to use PhotoShop or other picture editing software. What I used to create my logo was an app for

Android called Photo Editor by dev.macgyver. It's the same app I also used to create my banner and all my thumbnails for videos. Which leads us to making a banner for your channel. When making a banner you want to, just like the logo, keep it simple. What you should do is create a one or two-way color scheme background. Then make sure to add your logo somewhere in the banner. Also, be sure to list what your channel is about with topic words or sentences. For example, my channel is about business, technology, and YouTube. So, in my banner I out the keywords "Business" "Technology" & "YouTube" along with my logo on a blue and black background. Also, optional choices you have for your banner is adding text with the URL for your website or adding text telling the days you upload like "New Videos Monday, Wednesday, & Friday!" or "Videos Daily!" are a few examples for what you can add. If you need to view an example, then check out my channel by going to youtube.com/devinstreet_youtubechannel.

2. Video Creation and Upload Process

Your first videos are the first huge steps to creating a potential six to eight-figure income YouTube channel that could become your job. Everything from what the videos will be about to your thumbnail and tags will be huge in determining the direction your channel will go.

2.1 Idea For Video

Obviously, you need an idea for your first video. Most people want to make their first video about their intro or their channel trailer, my first video ever was my channel trailer. I would highly discourage doing this as your first video and it was one of my biggest mistakes. After at least 10 videos you could make a channel trailer but don't make it your first video because when creating a channel trailer you will want to use examples from other videos to get people to subscribe and you can't do that if you don't have any videos to use as an example. Secondly, you should NEVER upload your YouTube intro publically. If you look at any big YouTube channel, you will not find one that has their intro as a public upload. No one is searching for intros to binge-watch and you yourself have never done that either. When creating videos you want to be creating gateways for people to find your channel and then lead them into watching more videos and eventually subscribing. So depending on the theme of your channel, go with a specific video on the topic you have a great knowledge about and that people are searching for. So for instance if I'm a gaming channel and I play Minecraft, one of the most searched for but also most saturated videos on YouTube, I don't want to just make a video about Minecraft in general. What you will want to do is make a specific video about Minecraft like Killing Endermen in Minecraft, something still getting significant searches but has a lot less competition. Just remember you cannot continuously switch the topics of your videos on your channel or you will never be able to grow.

So if you're uploading two or three Minecraft videos at first and then start uploading vlogs and TV show reviews, you will be hurting your channel badly.

2.2 Creating The Video

Once you have the idea of the video created, it's time to shoot it. But first, since this is your first video, you will likely want to use a script or at least an outline. If you're using a script be sure not to make it obvious that you are using a script. If you choose to use an outline, make sure to stay on topic with the outline and don't get off track. I use outlines in most my videos and make sure not to go off topic of the outline and to stay on a straight path of how I want the video to go but I do make sure to make it natural and have an improv feel to it.

One key thing you need to do is already know what the title of your video is before you even record it. This is because if you mention the title of your video within the video, it will be in the closed captions, which will tell YouTube what your video is titled is what the video is actually about. This goes along with triple-keywording with your description and tags but we will talk about that later when we get to tagging and writing a description.

When recording the video, don't be nervous. This is your first. It's not going to be perfect. You will improve and that's what your first videos are for, to help you improve your video creating abilities. Just try your best and remember that video editing can fix most things.

2.3 Editing The Video

When it comes to editing, it will come down to two things, software, and experience. Each person edits their videos differently and has their own style to how they edit and what they used to accomplish that. Some people love being as high tech as possible and want to be given every possible option to make their video perfect. Others prefer an extremely laid back editing style of simple editing on their smartphone. Others go for whatever is free and available to them. And there are a few that are still using the same exact video editing software that they have been using for ten years because they feel they have mastered their current software and don't want to learn anything new. Everyone has their own style and so do you. I can't tell you how you should edit your videos and what with, that is your decision to make. What I can tell you are my opinions for the best video editing software out there and a couple of tips for editing your video.

If you are looking for the best of the best, I recommend getting Adobe Premiere Pro or Final Cut Pro. These are your best and easiest to master video editing software on desktop.

But if you are looking for a budget option on desktop then I recommend Blender and DaVinci Resolve. They closely resemble the high quality that you would receive with Adobe Premiere Pro or Final Cut Pro but they are free softwares.

And if you are on mobile the three apps I would recommend would be Kinemaster, the app I actually use to edit my videos on, PowerDirector, or iMovie. All three of these are great apps if you want to edit videos on your phone.

Next up, I have a good amount of tips for you when you are video editing. The first being to remember to edit your video at the end for end screens to added later when uploaded to YouTube. The last thing you want to do is have end cards hiding what is on your video to where the viewer can't see it. Remember that at the longest, you can have end screens for the last 20 seconds of your video but you don't have to make it 20 seconds if it's not necessary but concurrently you will want to give the viewer time to click on an end screen.

You will want to add music to your video to set tones and keep your audience engaged. The most important thing to remember when adding music to your video is you don't want the sound to overpower your voice and it's a good idea to use only instrumental music and no vocal music. When you are picking out the music you want to use, pick something that works with the tone of your video and with your personality and remember the music must be copyright free or you have the rights to use the music. If you are talented, you can even make your own music to go with your videos. Just try it out and see what you can do.

You will also need to change visuals frequently. You can't stare into a camera for 15 minutes and talk to it without some watch time drop off. Be sure to use animations, stock footage, and stock photos to spice up what is being viewed and increase the audience retention.

Another thing you will want to do is to be careful with color grading and adjustments as well. When doing color grading make it look pleasing to the viewer. Don't make your skin extremely red or too pale, but a nice balance.

Also, remember to cut out awkward silence in the video. It is so important to do this because I watch so many videos were the creator can be taken up to 10 seconds of not doing anything before saying something and this is so hard for me to watch because I know that these are the kinds of signs sent to viewers as a chance to leave the video and watch something else, killing the creator's watch time.

Take these tips and mix it with your own style and you will be an editing master. Just remember it will take practice. Over time you will get better and faster at editing your videos. I myself get better daily.

When it's time to export your video, be sure to export the video in the highest quality, the highest bit rates, and best frame rate you can get so that your video looks even more visually pleasing when uploaded to YouTube.

2.4 Creating The Thumbnail

The thumbnail and title of a video are what triggers a viewer to click or skip most videos. A thumbnail could end up deciding if you get more views, subscribers, and money for channel. Everyone chooses different styles for thumbnails but there are some important things to know when creating a thumbnail.

For your thumbnails, you will want to have a uniform style for your thumbnails with the same fonts, colors, your face, and other things so that people can distinguish which video is yours quickly. This is important because if someone likes your videos and wants to watch more, they can look in the suggested videos and quickly pick out your videos, increasing a watch session.

Another thing to do is to make sure the thumbnail relate to the title and video. If the thumbnail looks random compared to what the content of the video is supposed to be about, viewers won't click on the video and if they even do, they may leave immediately.

Another thing to do is to never use the same thumbnail for more than one video! It may seem like an obvious thing but many people will use the same thumbnail for each video in a series they create. That is the worst thing to do because it makes it hard for the viewer to distinguish between which videos they have watched and videos they haven't watched.

Another thing you would love to do is be sure to use your face in your thumbnail. The reason for this is statistics show that using a face in a thumbnail makes the thumbnail at least three times more clickable. This is because when the human brain sees a face, they have a psychological and emotional connection that makes them more likely to click.

The next thing you will want to do with your thumbnails is make sure it stands out from your competition. What I would recommend is going to the search and searching a possible video title that you would make and check out the videos and thumbnails that come up and figure out how you can stand out compared to the others.

Finally, one of the number one rules in creating a thumbnail is to never trick viewers with an event that doesn't show up in the video. False clickbait is the last thing you would want to do with a thumbnail.

2.5 Uploading The Video

Congratulations, your video has been filmed, edited and exported and the video's thumbnail has been created. Now it's time to upload it to YouTube. This will be one of the biggest steps in the process and will basically decide if your video will get the tons of views you are hoping for or if it will get any views at all. You'll read about that more in a second but first type in the title that you already planned out before you even recorded the video and upload the thumbnail you created and then let's talk about the description.

2.6 Video Description

The description of a video is one of the four SEO tools YouTube uses to rank your video. In my opinion, besides closed captions, it is the least import for ranking your video but you still need to put in significant time to craft the perfect description that will rank you the highest and generate subscribers and even sales on products and more followers on social media platforms.

You will want to have your title in your description too. It is important to have a keyword phrase you are targeting and have that in your title, description, and tags. It is recommended you put this keyword phrase as your title and then have it as the first thing in your description because when YouTube looks at the description, they take what is first as being more important over what comes later on in the description. Also, remember to include all the keywords in your description that you will also be using in your tags.

One thing to keep in mind when you are writing the beginning of your description is that only around the first 120 characters will be shown in search. While this has become less and less important over the years because fewer people read the description when they are searching for a video to click on and more people are using mobile than desktop, it is still something to keep in my because it could be the difference in getting that one new subscriber or missing out on them.

Another thing you will have to do when creating a description is to leave a link to subscribe in your description. Below is an example of how I included a link in my description to get people to subscribe, just in case they skipped the subscribe button and end screen but read the description.

Build your online presence! - Subscribe → https://goo.gl/yYotVW

Share this Video on Facebook, Twitter, etc!

As you can see I also ask them to share the video on Facebook, Twitter, and other platforms because this creates more leads I can get to my video, the more watch time, views, and channel growth I can get.

A great thing for gaining much watch time and help your videos SEO score, you will want to leave links to relevant videos and playlist in your description. This will increase how long someone watches you, boost your watch time, expands their session watch time, and could eventually lead to convincing them to subscribe.

The number one thing to do when writing a description is to always include affiliate links. This is one thing I do in each of my descriptions and if you don't know what they are, I will be talking about them in a later chapter and telling you how they can make you a significant amount of cash.

You will also want to leave links to all your social medias like Instagram, Twitter, and Facebook that are associated with your YouTube channel because the bigger you build your following there, the more traffic you can create to your YouTube channel.

Also, leave a link to your website if you have one for the same reasons as social medias.

Another thing I do occasionally in my description is encourage people to comment on the video by asking them a question and asking them to share the video sharing the video. This will increase engagement and trust for the viewer with your channel and the shares will also be another traffic source to get more people to watch your videos.

You should also add to your description a small section where you can explain what your channel is about and tell your story in it. This will help the viewer with grasping the idea of what your channel is about and give them a broad understanding of what your channel can offer them in terms of value that can be another attempt at getting them to subscribe. I think this is a great thing that you should have saved as a template to paste into each of your descriptions.

2.7 Video Tags

After finishing your description, it's time to add some tags to your videos. Before you even start tagging, you should have TubeBuddy, a YouTube browser extension, installed and be ready to use. To get TubeBuddy go to www.tubebuddy.com/devinstreet. The reason you need TubeBuddy is it's going to help you create your tags and choose more efficient and searchable tags to boost your video. Once TubeBuddy is installed go to the tags section in "Edit Video" and click the new "Explore" button that has now been added with TubeBuddy. Then the first thing you should do is type in your most searchable keyword phrase from your title into the "Explore" bar. For instance, if your title is "10 Ways To Raise Your Grades - How To Get Better Grades" then you would to type "How To Get Better Grades" or "Get Better Grades" into the "Explore" bar. Not only is this going to break down how good of a tag this may or may not be by telling you the amount of searches and competition for the tag but it will also give you related tags that you should use along with the one you are "exploring." This is important because TubeBuddy is giving you all the similar tags that people are searching for in the topic of your video. This will increase the areas your videos are showing up in search and give you more watch time to rank higher in searches. Just be sure that the tags relate to your video. This could hurt the average percentage of the video watched and YouTube also doesn't allow you to add unrelated tags and could lead to your video or channel being taken down.

Also, remember that the order of your tags matter. YouTube prioritizes the tags at the top and sees the tags at the bottom as less important. So, when adding tags, be sure to order them in what you think is the most searchable order. If you want to change the order of the tags, TubeBuddy offers a feature the lets you reorder your tags. Also, after the video is published and has been being viewed for weeks or months, some of your tags may start to rank in search. TubeBuddy will tell you which tags rank and what number they rank. Along with this, TubeBuddy has an option to auto-sort the tags by rank. It's useful and has helped me to take videos already doing well and make them rank higher.

Also remember to order your tags from which ones you think to be most relevant to least relevant. Along with this, you will want to order tags to where ones that are ranking high in search will be at the top and ones not ranking are at the bottom. TubeBuddy has a really great feature to help you do this.

2.8 Monetization

Author's Note: I wrote this part of the book before the YouTube Partner Program Changes and it is not applicable anymore for new channels starting out. Hopefully, this book doesn't become too outdated overtime as YouTube evolves but I did want to point out that now to monetize your channel with YouTube AdSense, you must earn 1,000 subscribers and 4,000 hours of watch time. Hopefully, you can reach this point soon!

Did I mention you're going to get to make money on your videos? Well, you can! What you will want to do is click on the "Monetization" tab and then you should see a tab that says "Monetize with ads." You will want to click that box and then choose what type of monetization you want. If you want to make the most money possible, choose "Monetize In All Countries." You will also be given options including "Non-skippable ads" and "Long Non-skippable ads." You will want to select these to make even more money but you have to remember this could keep people from sticking around to watch the video. One other way to make even more is that if your video is ten minutes or longer, you will have the option to place as breaks within the video. When utilized correctly, they can make you much money. But if done wrong, you could see huge drops in audience retention.

2.9 Cards

Cards can be one of the most important things to keeping a viewer's watch session going and continuing to binge-watch your videos. With cards, you are either are great with them or disastrous. When I first started YouTube, I was horrible at card placement. I didn't know where to place them and just put them in random spots. In all my studying of YouTube, there was nowhere to teach me about cards. It's like everyone just looks over them and doesn't see them as important. With this random placing strategy, I was getting a click rate of around 2%. Obviously, this is a bad click rate no matter what sort of thing you are talking about. But then I finally sat down and created a strategy and this book is the first place I'm sharing that strategy.

Firstly, you will want to put a card between two and four seconds of the video starting. As soon as the video starts the viewer is making immediate judgments of you as a person, the video resolution quality, the audio quality, and they are trying to decide if your video will solve their problem or not. All these things get addressed around the first few seconds of the video (if you're doing your videos correctly). If they decided that the video is not going to bring value then they are going to want to leave the video. This is where you create an escape for that viewer with a card. With this card, I recommend using a video suggestion of a video like the topic of the current video.

Secondly, you will want to put a card around the 30-second mark of the video. The reason I do this is with that first judgment I just talked about, many people decided the video is for them and they continue to watch. But by the time they reach the 30-second mark, they realize the video is not for them. Once again, just like the first card, you want to create an escape to another video. Also, like the first card, you will want to choose a similar video to the current one the viewer is watching.

The third and fourth cards are important and there is a simple way to increase click on these two cards. All you have to do is simply mention things that create a call to action. For instance, in my series about creating a WordPress website for free, I mentioned my own website in many of the videos. Every time I mentioned my website I would add a card that would direct people to my website to use it as a visual example if my video was not already offering that for them. This works the same way with mentioning a past video. I'm not going to talk that much about having a website along with your YouTube channel in this book but it is extremely important and I plan to release another book soon centered around WordPress websites and definitely want to have a section dedicated to the relationship between YouTube and a website.

Finally, the last card can be one of the most important cards because it can continue a watch time session. This card should work like an end screen. And just like an end screen, it should only appear during the final 20-second spans of the video. The best part about the card is that if in the video you began to wrap up before the final 20 seconds, then you can move the card to that point which differs from an end screen which only allows for up to the final 20 seconds. You can also put this card a few seconds after the end screens appear so that if the viewer does like any of the end screen available, then they can click the card.

That's all the information I can give about cards as I'm still discovering how to grow even more with cards but here are all the tips I can give on the topic:

- Have a card available immediately when the video starts for viewers who will automatically leave
- Make sure to have another card right behind for those few viewers who decide to stick

around but then realize the video is not for them

- Plan one to three cards in advance of recording your video so that you can mention it in the video and add the cards later as a call to action
- Utilize the final card as an and screen
- Get opinions of your audience through the poll cards
- If you have a website, use cards to increase traffic to the video
- Use cards to increase monetization

2.10 End Screens

End Screens are the best way to extend the session watch time, gain more views on your videos, and get subscribers. It's simple and it's and I'll tell you all about it here.

Why I love End Screens so much is because unlike the previous annotations used before End Screens, they work on mobile. That is so important because over half of viewers on YouTube are now coming from mobile devices like phones and tablets. Another reason I love End Screens is that they are so easy to implement. If you look at YouTube videos from 3 or 4 years ago, you can see how YouTubers manually added the thumbnails to certain videos they wanted you to add next. Many would have a video they recommend to their audience and their most recent video.

The problem with this was that their most recent video was always changing and recommend a video was great either because every viewer was different and most had already seen the recommended video. But with End Screens, everything is put in automatically and never the same for every viewer on any day. Now when you have a new video, that becomes your most recent video being suggested and YouTube decides which video is better for the viewer to watch next based mostly on watch history of your channel.

End Screens bring in significant amount of my views for my videos, which is good because I am increasing the watch time session and means viewers are binge-watching my content. And it's simple to get people to use End Screens.

First, you need should give a call to action. In my videos, I say at the end "If you enjoyed this video then be sure to watch some of my other videos and subscribe." By saying this I am reminding the viewer to use the End Screens that are appearing in front of them while I say this and giving them the option of watching other videos, via my video or playlist End Screens, or to subscribe, via the subscribe End Screen.

When you do your Ends Screens you will want to add both the recent and recommended video End Screens and the subscribe End Screen. If you think you can fit it and it doesn't overwhelm the viewer, add a playlist End Screen also for the topic the video is about. This will get you the most views, subscribers, and increase watch time session.

Throughout uploading YouTube videos, I have experimented a lot with how the End Screens should appear. For a while, I used a template for the End Screens but quickly changed due to it having zero flexibility for me to change things when I need to.

Next, I tried fading in a blur for the last 20 seconds of the video and having the End Screens appear. I used this for a while, but changed it because I thought it looked unprofessional and lazy.

Finally, I created a hybrid between the two with a half template for important messages and social medias and the other half for the End Screens. Here is an example picture for context.

So that's been my relationship with End Screen and here are a few tips to remember when doing End Screens:

- Have a call to action for the End Screens like "Check out some more videos and subscribe"
- ALWAYS use the subscribe, recommended video, and recent video End Screens and the playlist End Screen if possible
- Remember that End Screens work on mobile and desktop (but not the YouTube TV App at the moment)
- Use a template, a blur, or hybrid to introduce your End Screens
- Be thankful for End Screens and that you don't have to use annotations

2.11 Subtitles/Closed Captions

Subtitles/Closed Captions are a great metadata source for SEO to rank your videos at the top of searches and drive more views to your YouTube videos. One of the best parts about Closed Captions is many people don't even add them to their videos which opens up the opportunity for you to outrank the competition with Captions.

YouTube does auto-generated subtitles for you but there is no sign of any punctuation in these subtitles at all. And, sometimes it doesn't even hear what you said or misspells what you said. For instance, whenever I say my name, instead of it putting "Devin" it generates "Devon".

I suggest taking what YouTube auto-generates for you and editing whatever mistakes you see and upload a new corrected version of the subtitles.

And remember when I said that Closed Captions will help you outrank other videos? Well here is exactly how you can do that. Many people don't even think of their title until it's time to upload the video. Before you even record your video, you need to know what the title of your video is going to be (remember to do your keyword research). And the reason is YouTube uses the captions as almost a secondary tagging system. Don't you think if the video has the same keyword phrase in the title, description, tags, and captions YouTube won't give it a high relevancy score? Remember YouTube sorts videos in search by relevance and ranks them by relevance and watch time. That's why I have a video with just a few hundred views ranking in between videos with hundreds of thousands and thousands of views pictured below.

does sub4sub work

About 8,270 results   ☰ FILTER

Does Sub for Sub on YouTube Actually Work? - Sub 4 Sub

Derral Eves ✔ · 107K views · 3 years ago

Does Sub for Sub on YouTube Actually **Work**? —Derral talks with fellow YouTube expert Tim Schmoyer for this fun and entertaining

CC

Does Sub4Sub Work?

Devin Street · 62 views · 5 months ago

Does Sub4Sub Work? Well in this video I'm going to be talk about Sub4Sub and if it works, if it's good for your channel, and the main

CC

Why YouTube Sub4Sub is BAD

Roberto Blake ✔ · 41K views · 2 years ago

Why YouTube **Sub4Sub** is BAD http://youtu.be/VMbngWvulAg If you're trying to get more YouTube subscribers, **Sub4Sub** is not the

2.12 Translations

Translations are a great way to increase views on your YouTube videos. Need proof? Well, 30% of my views come just from India. Now I'm not an expert on translations but I will tell you to get your titles, descriptions, and most importantly, captions translated into as many languages as possible. If you believe you have the money then I would suggest getting professional translations for the top three to four languages. Not much else to say about translations besides that it will definitely increase your views.

2.13 Advance Settings

The last thing in the upload process is the advanced settings. While the advanced settings do not help in your success on YouTube, they are still important with categorization and legal jargon found here. I'll just list a few points on what you should do in the advanced settings:

- Categorized your video correctly
- Choose to correct license and rights ownerships based on if you want other people to remix your video
- Make sure video is available on all platforms
- Allow Embedding
- Select Correct Language
- Make video stats public
- Allow community contributions
- Check paid promotion if applicable

3. Managing Your YouTube Channel

So now you have created your YouTube channel, know exactly how to create, upload, and optimize your videos for getting the most views and subscribers. Now it is time to learn to manage your channel like a brand and business. That's what our goal was in the beginning, right? Turning your channel into your business and full-time job by managing it to build a following and make plenty of cash in the process.

3.1 Engaging With Your Audience

As a content creator, it's not only your job to create content for your audience but to also make each individual feel special as if you are creating all your content just for them. This includes engaging and interacting with the individual as much as possible The next few chapters are going to be about all the ways you can engage with your audience, as it is key to manage your channel.

3.2 The Power Of Commenting

Commenting on YouTube is so powerful. The first thing you will want to do is to comment on your own video with a link to another video you want to send traffic to. You will want to pin this comment to the top of your videos so when people get to the comments sections, your comment is the first comment to show up and get the viewer's attention to take action. An example of below:

Notice how the comment has been pinned to the top so it will always stay there no matter how the comments are being sorted. Also, notice how I have bolded the text by putting asterisks around it to draw more attention. Finally, also noticed I have used a Google Shorten URL using https://goo.gl/ so that I can track how many clicks the URL gets and just to make the link look nicer.

Next up, you will want to interact with each commenter on your videos, well unless they're just a spammer trying to get subscribers. You want every commenter to feel special and that you actually cared enough to reply to them. You could use anything from just a single emojis to a couple sentences or a paragraph. It makes the viewer feel valuable and keeps subscribers coming back to each video to watch as much as they can and liking and commenting. If you love their comment then be sure to use the heart feature to heart their comment so it is featured to everyone right below the pinned comment.

Another great way to use comments is if a commenter is having a problem or looking for something. For instance if someone commented on my video about gaining subscribers and they asked something like "How can I get more views to convert to subscribers?" then I could comment with a shortened link to one of my videos about getting more views. Not only have I helped solve their problem and gained a subscriber but I've also sent them to go watch more of my videos and anyone else who sees the comment could click the link and watch the video. It is an easy way to help your views while getting more views.

3.3 Promoting Your Channel Across Social Media

If you want to get noticed on YouTube and want to grow faster, you're going to have to give your video views a little push with some extra exposure on social media platforms. You're going to want to use as many platforms as possible to send people to your video from everywhere. You should be using Twitter, Instagram, Facebook, Snapchat, LinkedIn, and promoting through blogging.

What you don't want to be doing is just using a social media account to spam about your YouTube videos. You want to build up strong following on those platforms and promoting videos when they come out. YouTube even offers you the ability to automatically Tweet about your new video when it comes out. Knowing the balance between offering value and spam is the key to growing.

Facebook groups can be powerful asset in getting views and watch time fast. You should join as many groups that are in your niche as possible. For instance, if your channel is about Star Wars Battlefront 2, then you will want to join all the Battlefront 2 Facebook groups and all the Star Wars groups and maybe even some gaming groups. Once you are into these groups please contribute and be active in the group before ever posting a link to your video. Get involved with everyone in the group and be known as a popular member of the group before posting video. You have to get them to trust you and know that you are sending them to something good. If you don't, then they won't click on any more of your links and could report you for spam.

3.4 Playlist

YouTube playlists are one of the most important parts of growing on YouTube and something a neglected for a long time.

When I finally started to use playlist more on my channel, I saw tremendous growth. Daily views tripled and quadrupled overnight. I began gaining subscribers ten times faster. Basically, playlist are one of the most important parts of YouTube.

The reason playlist are so great is not only do playlist earn each individual video watch time minutes, but also the playlist gets accumulates its own watch time and increase a watch session for a viewer where they only watch you.

Now you do have to be careful with playlist though. One bad video that doesn't fit into the theming will lead to them abandoning the entire playlist which will mean they are not watching all the videos and they are also ending their watch session which will penalize you.

I recommend sticking to a strong theme with a playlist and if you know that a video is bad and will cause people to leave, then don't put the video in the playlist.

Also, remember to give great carefully worded descriptions for each of these playlists because a big goal with a playlist is trying to rank the playlist in search. If you can rank a playlist in search then you can get many subscribers, views, and massive amounts of watch time.

You will also want to suggest playlist in descriptions of videos, video cards, and in the video end screens. It is very valuable and you will definitely want to use it.

Playlist are your greatest friend on YouTube and you will want to use them as much as possible. Playlist even get counted by YouTube as new content being created/uploaded so it will help favor you in the algorithm because you are posting more frequently.

3.5 Demonetization

One of the most feared thing on YouTube now is demonetization. Demonetization is when YouTube sees a video as not advertiser-friendly for inappropriate or spammy content and make the decision to limit or entirely halt ads on the video.

While the artificial intelligence that decides if videos should be demonetized is getting better daily, many of my videos and other perfectly safe channel's videos have been demonetized.

So when you get demonetized you will have to go through your video to make sure that there is nothing controversial in it and then ask for it to be reviewed by a human reviewer.

You will also need to figure out how to avoid getting demonetized. Try to stay away from language, violence, politics, and even spammy or sketchy tags like with my video that got demonetized used the tag "how to make money fast for free."

Next, you will probably want to set up other ways to make income so you are not relying on just YouTube ads for your income. Anyone who relies on YouTube ads to make their living is living on the thinnest sheet of ice for a career and I just hate when many YouTubers complain about having to get an extra job to support themselves when they have half a million subscribers or more. You don't need near that much to make a fair amount of money with some helpful ways in the next few chapters.

3.6 Affiliate Marketing

Affiliate marketing is one of the most powerful and my favorite way to make money online. If you don't know what affiliate marketing is, get prepared because it is pretty amazing.

Affiliate marketing is where you as a creator and influencer can get links from companies that you can use to send your audience to buy products or try out trials to what the company has to offer. When they use the link and purchase something or try the trial then you get paid, usually with a commission from a percentage of the products price.

So let's say that you are in an affiliate partnership with a computer company that gives you 20% commission on each computer you get someone to buy. So if you can get only one out of thousands of people to buy a $1000 computer then you make $200. Cool right?

The best thing is almost every company offers an affiliate program. I recommend using the Amazon Affiliate Program and MagicLinks, a site that gives you affiliate links to thousands of different products on hundreds of products. You can go to https://www.magiclinks.org/rewards/referral/devin stree/ sign up for MagicLinks!

3.7 Making Brand Deals

Brand deals are a great way to make money on YouTube to help make YouTube your full-time job while bringing value to your audience to help them. I myself have even been able to do a few brand deals with companies and I can promise that they pay off well if you know how to do them.

So how do you get these great brand deals? Well, first you need to know what company you want to do a deal with. Brand deals are not cash grabs, you need to bring value to your audience! So before you go jumping at a deal offered to you, you have to ask "Will this help my viewers if they buy this?" If the answer is no, then don't do the deal. I have had deals offered to me that didn't even make sense for me to do because it wasn't in my niche at all. That's why you see me doing deals with brands like Morning Fame and TubeBuddy because they have the same goals I do, to help people grow on YouTube.

So how do you negotiate a brand deal? Well if a brand has already contacted you or connected in some way then a great way to take advantage to get a deal. If not, just find a way to contact them. I recommend emailing them, it's the most professional way to contact a company. Below is an example of an email I sent in reply to a company that began deal negotiations and eventually landed me a nice deal.

Yeah ███████,

I would be interested in creating an entire series and playlist dedicated to , along with promotion across all my other social medias, featuring ███████ in my upcoming podcast, writing articles about ███████ on my website, and advertising in the my company's bi-yearly Internet marketing magazine. This would be a two year promotional deal and in return I would like a , equity in ███████, and cash but you will have me locked in for two years as a major sponsor and as a minority owner, I would make sure to grow as much as I possibly could.

Let me know what you think,
Devin Street

While I definitely didn't get everything asked, as I purposely asked for too much in the first proposal so when the deal value was brought down I would still be treated fairly. This was one of my most successful email proposing a brand deal and all it took was contact them about it. The deal would have never happened if I didn't send the email so don't wait around for brands to come to you if they haven't already. Go to them!

Finally, once a brand deal has been made, see it as a relationship with a company. Don't make a deal a one time thing. Do more deals after your first one and build a strong relationship with the company. Long-term relationships are always better than a one night stand, and I'm not talking about dating.

3.8 Selling Merchandise

Merchandise is another way to make a good amount of cash on YouTube. Merchandise can be anything you think your audience would love. That could be t-shirts, hats, keychains, phone cases, or posters. If your audience is willing to buy it, then you should probably be selling it.

The merchandise also doesn't have to be about your channel but instead could be about your niche. While my YouTube channel is about growing on YouTube, Twitter, Instagram, and other platforms, I sell motivation t-shirts and have even taken design that I created for Instagram pictures and turned it into t-shirts.

The possibilities for selling merchandise is endless and one great thing is you don't even have to be in charge of making the merchandise and shipping it. Websites like Spreadshirt and Shopify can easily help you with setting up a store to sell your merchandise. You can even put it on Amazon and use your affiliate links to get even more money from the sales. The bottom line is that merchandise is something you will want to look into.

3.9 Create A Online Course

An online course is another great way to get your audience significant value and gets you a lot of cash. This one will take a lot more of your time because you need to create a grand package for the course with exclusive videos, articles, templates, walkthroughs, books, downloads, and other great exclusive resources to sell the idea that they will be buying something powerful.

Take your niche and come up with a workshop class that people would want to learn something from and give them all the resources mentioned to help them to get a true specific teaching of the material. For instance, at the moment I am working on a course to teach SEO Ranking on YouTube and what goes into getting your video #1 on searches.

Another great example of a great course is one created by Roberto Blake called "The YouTube Starter Kit." It comes with thumbnail packs, channel art templates, end card templates, lower third templates, font downloads, and ideas for YouTube videos. It is over $1500 in value and he sells it for $99 and many have bought it.

So spend 1 to 2 weeks working on a course that your audience would buy and you could be bringing in thousands of dollars if it's good enough.

3.10 Offer A Service

Chances are if you are a YouTuber that you are a creative and have some great talents. Since that is the case, maybe you can create a service around one of your many talents to sell to your audience. You're likely a pretty good photo and video editor considering all your time working with creating great thumbnails and wonderful videos so you can offer a service to your audience to edit their videos or photos. You could also offer this on Fiverr and get people to buy there.

You might also have a great voice because you likely use your voice for YouTube. You can use your talented voice as a service by offering voice-overs, singing, and being a voice actor.

You can even offer to be an actor in someone else's video if you are good at acting and have shown the skills for it on your channel.

3.11 Fan-Funding Through Patreon

Another great way to make money is by just asking your audience to donate to you. Many people don't like to ask their audience to give to them but many of your viewers feel you have helped them so much that they want to give back to you. Instead of just them donating to you, give back to them when they donate by using Patreon.

If you don't know what Patreon is, it's a service where your audience can donate to you on a monthly basis or donate every time you release new content. The best part of Patreon is you can have rewards for your donators based on how much they donate with different reward tiers.

So maybe if they donate $2 per month they get a shoutout at the end of everyone one of your videos. If they donate $10 per month then you could give them access to exclusive monthly videos. If they donate $15 per month you could FaceTime with them each month for an hour or so and answer questions with them. And if they donate $20 per month you could have them be in one of your videos in some way. That is just one example of how you can reward your Patreon members but you can set the price and rewards to whatever you think is best for you to make the most profit and give them most value.

Final Thoughts

As I begin to close this book, there is so much more I would love to talk about. There are endless ideas about YouTube I would love to keep putting in this book but I have been writing it for over 8 months now and I realize I need to just put it out there instead of continuing to work on it. Which leads me to my next point.

At the end of the day, you could always continue to work on small little things for your YouTube video but you have to just get it out there because that one little second where the video isn't extremely perfect is not going to hurt your watch time. DON'T BE PERFECT. With social media, quantity will always trump quality. Everything doesn't have to be perfect but you do have to show up. The YouTuber who is putting out 8 imperfect videos a month is going to bet the YouTube who puts out 1 perfect video. So I challenge you to get out as much content as possible and focus on growing as fast as you can and never look back. I wish you the best of luck on your road to becoming a successful YouTuber.

The YouTuber Dictionary

- **Accumulated Watch Time:** all the total watch time on a video by all the viewers who have watched it. It is a key factor to ranking videos in search and having your video suggested.

- **Affiliate Marketing:** a marketing arrangement by which an online retailer pays a commission to a YouTube creator for traffic or sales generated from its referrals via custom referral links.

- **Average Watch Time Duration:** the average amount of time a viewer will watch a video. The longer the time, the better the video will perform.

- **Demonetization:** when ads are no longer played on a video and it no longer earns money. Happens when video is not advertiser-friendly.

- **Monetization:** the ability to place ads on your YouTube videos via Google AdSense and get paid a portion of the ads cost.

- **Playlist:** a group of videos together that play in a certain order. Helpful in getting much watch time at once through binge-watching.

- **Relevancy:** is how closely a video's title, description, tags, and subtitles match a keyword phrase that is searched.

- **SEO**: stands for search engine optimization and includes the practices to follow to get your videos ranked in search.

- **Subtitles:** words displayed at the bottom of the video that transcribes or translates what is being spoken in the video. Helpful for reaching more viewers and increasing SEO.

- **Suggested Video:** a video being suggested to a viewer because the video they are currently watching or their watch history.

- **Thumbnail:** the picture that is shown with a video title before it is clicked on. Important for getting more people to click on your video.

- **Video Cards:** a clickable icon that appears in the top right corner of a video that can take viewers to another video, a playlist, a website, or let them make a donation.

- **Video Tags:** a single or a string of keywords used to help YouTube with determining what the video is about so YouTube knows when to show it in search. Extremely important to SEO and video relevancy.

- **Watch Session:** the time from when a viewer starts watching videos on YouTube to when they stop watching. You can get rewarded for starting a session and penalized for ending one.

- **Watch Time:** the amount of time a video is watched by a single viewer. Important for accumulated watch time.

<u>Need Help Growing?</u>

Online Entrepreneurs Media
Can Help You!

Online Entrepreneurs Media, LLC. is dedicated to helping you grow your online presence at no initial monetary cost! We can help you grow today. Just contact us through email or visit our website.

What are you waiting for? You're future starts now!

onlineentrepreneursmedia@gmail.com

Best Tool For YouTube!

It's Called TubeBuddy

TubeBuddy can grow your channel 10x faster and save you thousands of dollars in time!

"TubeBuddy has completely transformed the way I manage my personal YouTube channel and my clients' channels!"
-Derral Eves

Get it today by going to the link below!

tubebuddy.com/devinstreet

Made in United States
Orlando, FL
23 May 2023

33408567R00050